GROW YOUR OWN INGREDIENTS
PASTA SAUCE!

CASSIE LIVERSIDGE

Sky Pony Press
New York

I would like to dedicate this book to George and Thomas.

Sky Pony Press books may be purchased in bulk at special discounts for sales promotion, corporate gifts, fund-raising, or educational purposes. Special editions can also be created to specifications. For details, contact the Special Sales Department, Sky Pony Press, 307 West 36th Street, 11th Floor, New York, NY 10018 or info@skyhorsepublishing.com.

Sky Pony® is a registered trademark of Skyhorse Publishing, Inc.®, a Delaware corporation.

Visit our website at www.skyponypress.com.

10 9 8 7 6 5 4 3 2 1

Printed in India

Library of Congress Cataloging-in-Publication Data

Liversidge, Cassie.
Pasta sauce! : grow your own ingredients / Cassie Liversidge.
p. cm.
ISBN 978-1-62087-533-9 (hardcover : alk. paper) 1. Vegetable gardening--Juvenile lit-erature. 2. Herb gardening--Juvenile literature. 3. Sauces--Juvenile literature. 4. Cooking (Vegetables)--Juvenile literature. I. Title.
SB324.L58 2013
635--dc23
2012041060

CONTENTS

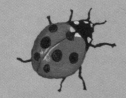

Introduction

Welcome! This book will help you to grow all of the fresh ingredients you need—along with the recipe—to cook the most delicious pasta dish you have ever tasted! Hopefully you will make so much pasta sauce that you will be able to put it in jars and give it to family and friends!

TOP TIPS TO GROWING SUCCESS!

This chart is a rough guide of when to sow the seeds and when to harvest your produce. Try to follow the instructions on the seed packet/label and be aware of your local weather, as it is important that the seeds and plants have the conditions they like so they can grow well.

	Jan	Feb	March	April	May	June	July	Aug	Sept	Oct	Nov	Dec
Garlic							▓	▓				
Onions						▓		▓				
Tomato							▓	▓	▓	▓		
Pepper						▓	▓		▓			
Basil				▓	▓	▓	▓	▓	▓	▓		

When to sow	▓
When to harvest	▓

Garlic and onions can be grown in pots if you need to. Just follow the instructions in the book and plant according to the size of your container. Not too many plants in a pot to allow them room to grow.

FERTILIZER and PLANT FOOD

Tomatoes and peppers love to be fed extra nutrients. You can either buy an organic tomato food from a garden center or use your own diluted worm tea if you have a wormery. Spraying the leaves with worm tea can also help keep bugs away! Adding your own home-grown compost (which is made from dead plant material from the bottom of a compost bin) will help to put more nutrients in to your soil, so your plants will grow bigger and stronger.

The WEATHER

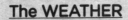

As a general tip, vegetables love the sun as this helps to warm the soil to germinate the seeds and ripen the fruits. So put them in as sunny a position as you can.

Tomatoes, peppers, and basil need nice, warm, sunny weather to grow and ripen and will not survive if there is a frost, so check your local weather forecast before they go outside. Onions and garlic don't mind the cold and are happy planted outside.

Leggy Seedlings!

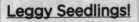

If your seedlings are getting leggy (a bit thin and tall) on your windowsill, you need to get them outside into either a greenhouse or somewhere covered. Or, if there is no danger of frost (check your local weather forecast) they can go directly outside.

Watering

Seedlings like to be kept moist but not soggy! They will not survive if they dry out! They are only little!

Make sure your containers/pots have holes in the bottom to allow water to drain.

Sometimes things go wrong but do not worry! Keep trying and learning, and you will get there! Have fun getting your hands dirty and nurturing your ingredients. Most of all, get ready to taste the best food in the world, because you will have grown it yourself!

GROW YOUR OWN PASTA SAUCE
TOMATOES

You will need . . .

Bush plum tomato seed. A great variety is Window Box Roma or Sweet Olive.

Potting soil (compost)

Small pots

Labels

Permanent marker

A watering can and a spray bottle (water sprayer)

A BIG POT

A sieve

You can sprinkle the soil with your hands if you don't have a sieve.

STEP 1

Fill the pots with potting soil. Give the pots two taps to let the soil settle and then sieve some finer compost until the pot is full. Gently level off the soil so it's nice and flat but don't push down.

Potting soil (compost)

STEP 2

Lay two seeds in each pot, then gently sieve a small amount of soil over the top.

STEP 3

Stand each pot in a saucer full of water and spray with water every day to keep the soil moist. Keep somewhere warm and sunny, like a window sill.

Label each pot.

STEP 4

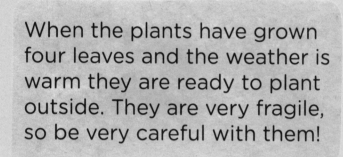

When the plants have grown four leaves and the weather is warm they are ready to plant outside. They are very fragile, so be very careful with them!

STEP 5

STEP 6

Make a hole in the soil.
Take the seedlings out of their pots and
carefully place one plant in each hole.
Push the soil around the
plant to make it firm.
Water well every day.

Top tip: Put me somewhere sunny and give me lots of tomato feed to get a bumper crop!

STEP 7

Watch as the flowers turn into green tomatoes and then ripen to red ones ready to be picked for your pasta sauce.

Tomato Jokes!
Why did the tomato blush?
Because he saw the salad dressing!

Why is a tomato round and red?
Because if it were long and green it would be a cucumber!

GROW YOUR OWN PASTA SAUCE
ONIONS

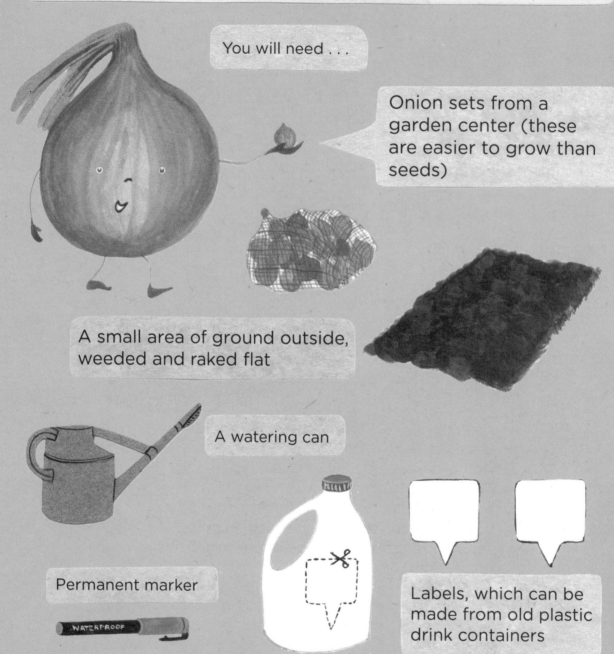

You will need . . .

Onion sets from a garden center (these are easier to grow than seeds)

A small area of ground outside, weeded and raked flat

A watering can

Permanent marker

WATERPROOF

Labels, which can be made from old plastic drink containers

STEP 1

Make a shallow trench about 1¼ in (3 cm) deep.

Place the onion sets in the trench pointy side up, 4 in (10 cm) apart.

STEP 2

Cover the onions with soil, just leaving the top pointing out. Write a label for the end of the row.

Water the onions regularly if it doesn't rain and keep the soil around the onions clear of weeds.

STEP 3

By midsummer and autumn they will be ready to harvest and make into pasta sauce!

Top Tip:
After you have harvested them they will store for weeks if you keep them somewhere dry.

Joke: What's round and white and giggles?
A tickled onion!

GROW YOUR OWN PASTA SAUCE
BASIL

You will need . . .

Sweet basil seed

Small pots

Spray bottle
(water sprayer)

Potting soil
(compost)

Labels

WATERPROOF

Permanent marker

BASIL SEED HERB

STEP 1

Fill the pots with potting soil (compost) and then smooth over so it is nice and flat.

Potting soil (compost)

STEP 2

Lay five seeds on the <u>top</u> of the soil (don't make a hole!) and sprinkle more soil over until you can't see the seeds. Label your pot.

Potting soil (compost)

STEP 3

Stand each pot in a saucer full of water and then keep them inside on a sunny windowsill and spray with water every day.

Top Tip: Germination (which means shooting or sprouting) of these seeds can take 2-3 weeks! So don't forget watering me. I am growing.

When I have grown lots of lovely smelling basil leaves I am ready to be picked for your pasta sauce. Try growing my herb friend Oregano too.

GROW YOUR OWN PASTA SAUCE
PEPPERS

You will need . . .

Sweet pepper seed

A watering can and a spray bottle (water sprayer)

Potting soil (compost)

A BIG POT

Small pots

Labels

Permanent markers

STEP 1

STEP 2

Lay two seeds in each pot, then gently sprinkle a small amount of soil over the seeds. Label each pot.

Top Tip: You put two seeds in each pot as only one seed may germinate.

STEP 3

Stand each pot in a saucer of water. Spray with water every day to keep the soil moist.

Keep somewhere warm and sunny, like a windowsill.

It can take 2–3 weeks for the seeds to sprout, so don't forget about me!

STEP 4

When you can see roots through the holes in the bottom of the pot it is time to give the plant more room to grow.

Fill a large pot with potting soil and carefully plant the peppers into the soil.

Keep in a greenhouse or somewhere warm and sunny. Water every day.

STEP 5

As the pepper plants grow, tie them to a stick or a cane to stop them from falling over.

When the sweet peppers are big enough, pick to use in your pasta sauce!

Top Tip: Give me lots of organic tomato feed to get lots of peppers!

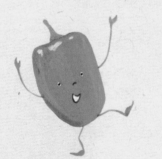

Joke: How can you tell a chili pepper from a regular pepper? The chilly one wears a shawl.

GROW YOUR OWN PASTA SAUCE
GARLIC

You will need . . .

A garlic bulb

We can be planted in the cold winter months to be harvested in the summer!

Labels

A small area of ground outside, weeded and raked flat

WATERPROOF

Permanent marker

A watering can

Make a deep trench in the soil. Break the garlic bulb into segments, which are called cloves, and plant them 4 in (10 cm) apart and 2 in (5 cm) deep. Cover with soil and label the ends of the row.

GARLIC

Keep removing any weeds and water the garlic if it doesn't rain.

When the leaves turn yellow I am ready to be harvested and used in your pasta sauce!

GARLIC

COOK YOUR OWN PASTA SAUCE

To cook a meal for four people, you will need your homegrown:

Pepper: One whole green, red, or yellow pepper

Basil: A bunch

Onion: One

Tomatoes: As many as you can harvest or about ten big handfuls

Garlic: You need half of a small bulb, or about four cloves

Saucepan

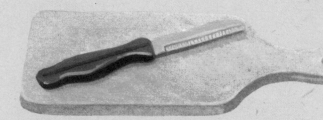

Chopping board and knife

OLIVE OIL

Frying pan and spatula

Pasta: Any shape and about ten big handfuls

STEP 1

Wash your hands and put an apron on. Ask an adult for help and always be very careful in the kitchen.

Ask an adult to cut the onion in half.

Then cut the ends off of the onion and peel the outer skin off.

Cut the onion into quarters and slice into little pieces, being very careful to keep your fingers out of the way. When finished, put to one side.

STEP 2

If your garlic is straight out of the ground it will be very fresh! Cut the stalk off and peel off the outer skin.

Cut the garlic bulb in half and use one half for this recipe. Chop the roots off. Wash under cold water. Then cut into tiny pieces.

If you have garlic that has been stored and is dried, peel off the outer skin of the bulb and find four cloves (segments). Peel each clove.

Chop off the top and bottom of each clove. Slice and cut into tiny pieces. Put to one side when finished.

STEP 3

Put the tomatoes in a colander and wash them under cold water. Cut all of the tomatoes in half. Put to one side when finished.

STEP 4

Wash the pepper. Ask an adult to cut the pepper into quarters.

Cut out the seeds and put these into a compost bin if you have one.

Cut the pepper into small pieces. When you have finished put to one side.

STEP 5

Wash the basil leaves under cold water. Pick the leaves off of the stems. Then tear the leaves into tiny bits.

All the ingredients are ready!

Basil

Chopped tomatoes

Chopped garlic

Chopped onion

Chopped pepper

STEP 6

Now it's time to get cooking! Ask an adult to help you.

Put the frying pan on the burner (which is the top of the stove or cooker) over a medium heat. Add a few drops of olive oil. Add the garlic and onions and stir until a light brown color.

STEP 7

Add the chopped tomatoes and one mug of water.

STEP 8

Simmer (which means cook gently) for about 15 minutes, stirring every so often. Add more water if the sauce is getting too thick.

STEP 9

While the sauce is cooking, put a saucepan of water onto another burner and bring to a boil (which means when it's bubbling a lot!).

STEP 10

Ask an adult to put the pasta into the boiling hot water. Cook for as long as the pasta label says, probably about 12 minutes if it is dried pasta.

STEP 11

Add the pepper to the tomato sauce and cook for 3 more minutes.

STEP 12

Ask an adult to strain the pasta when it's ready. Put into a big bowl.

STEP 13

Pour the pasta sauce over the pasta and mix well.

STEP 14

Sprinkle the basil over the top.

Serve your pasta on a plate and add some cheese if you would like.

Then EAT the most delicious pasta sauce ever!

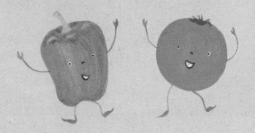

ACKNOWLEDGMENTS

I would like to thank the following for all their help and support in the production of this book: Peter Liversidge, George and Thomas Liversidge, Isabel Atherton (Creative Authors), Levin Haegele, Frank Williams, Keris Salmon, teachers, pupils, and gardening parents at Chisenhale Primary School, Paul the Gardener, Jim Bliss, James Huggins, Jo de Guia, and of course all at Sky Pony Press, especially Talia Ergas and Julie Matysik.

For more information about growing your own please see my website: www.cassieliversidge.com

You can also follow me on Facebook
www.facebook.com/Grow-Your-Own-Ingredients
Twitter @Cass_Liversidge

About the Author

Cassie Liversidge is a fine artist and mom of two young boys, as well as an avid gardener and cook. She has been developing an "Edible Playground" at her son's school in East London, and the idea for this book grew out of that. Cassie was lucky to be raised in the country, where her parents owned a plant nursery, so growing is something she once took for granted and now loves to share with adults and children alike. Cassie believes that if a child is given the knowledge and confidence to grow their own food it will be a vital tool for changing the way future generations live in a more sustainable way. This is her first children's book.

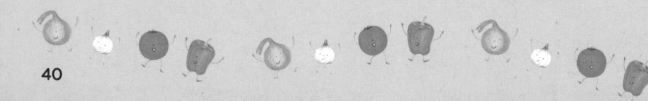